Play Better TENNIS

JOYCE HUME

Series editor: Paul Wade

PELHAM BOOKS
LONDON

Produced by
Breslich & Foss
Golden House
28-31 Great Pulteney Street
London W1R 3DD

Concept: Team Wade
Fitness Consultant: Gordon Richards MBE
Design: Roger Daniels
Photographs: Tommy Hindley
Editor: Judy Martin

First published in Great Britain by
Pelham Books Ltd
44 Bedford Square
London WC1B 3DP
1986

British Library Cataloguing in Publication Data

Hume, Joyce
    Play better tennis : 50 star tips.
    1. Tennis
    I. Title   II. Richards, Gordon
    796.342'2   GV995
    ISBN 0-7207-1683-7

Typeset by Lineage Ltd, Watford
Originated and printed by
Toppan Printing Co. (S) Pte. Ltd., Singapore

Contents

Introduction

Tennis has exploded as a major international sport since the game officially went professional in 1968. While the USA has dominated in the past as the world's most powerful tennis nation, Sweden, Czechoslovakia and West Germany now present a consistent challenge. Sweden's Bjorn Borg surely still ranks as the all-time tennis phenomenon, while the more recent triumph of Boris Becker helped to put West Germany squarely on the tennis map. The sheer thrill and entertainment of top-class tennis involves a world-wide audience in each major tournament and through television we can follow the skills of the tennis superstars all year round. But this book is designed to slow down the pace, so that instead of just marvelling at their power and versatility, we can learn from them as well.

I have specially chosen 50 exciting pictures of the world's greatest players in action, from the collection of Tommy Hindley, the British Lawn Tennis Association's official photographer. From these I have analysed the classic shots and tactical skills the players employ; and from my coaching experience I have warned against the common errors that occur when these techniques are attempted by less practised players. To ensure a good start, I have also assembled some tips on choosing the right equipment for your game and hints on match preparation, whether for your regular Thursday night doubles or for the finals of your club championship.

As you must know from both watching and playing, tennis is a physically demanding game. You need stamina to stay in a long match, but speed to retrieve a wide ball; you need power for baseline shots and serves, touch for volleys and flexibility to change direction quickly, both in your own movement and in wielding the racket. I am grateful to fitness expert Gordon Richards for supplying an exercise routine that demands effort, certainly, but not too much time, so you can get into peak condition for tennis without losing your hours for practice. I would also like to thank series editor Paul Wade, for practical assistance and encouragement during the writing of this book.

Each photograph is chosen to demonstrate a particular aspect of the game. Whether the featured player is male or female, this does not imply that any technique is exclusive to the men's or women's game, or inappropriate to your own repertoire.

I hope that you can all learn equally from the skills of these very fine players and with the aid of this handbook, will feel properly equipped to 'Play Better Tennis'.

Joyce Hume

Chris Evert Lloyd

Classic forehand drive

The game of tennis demands many attributes of its exponents. One of the most significant is control
● of the racket
● of the rallies
● of temperament
Chris Evert Lloyd's type of game personifies total control. From this typical forehand you can sense Chrissie's single-mindedness and the care behind the shot. Her mind is obviously working out the rally in progress and her racket simply puts her thoughts into practice. This shot is part of the strategy of moving her opponent around the court, gradually working her out of position with immaculate precision and cool calculation.

COMMON FAULTS
1 Hitting the ball off the back foot. No pace can then be put on the shot as your weight is falling backwards.
2 Dropping the head of the racket, producing a scooped, uncontrolled shot.

WHEN TO PLAY
This basic forehand is one of the 'bread and butter' shots of the game, in particular the mainstay of a rally played from the back of the court. It can be a safe shot, played calmly and without undue pressure, testing your opponent's capabilities.

It can also be a forcing shot aimed at wearing down your opponent's resistance. This should be played both down the line and cross-court with equal ease.

HOW TO PLAY
1 Make sure your Eastern grip allows the palm of the hand to give extra support to the racket. The Eastern grip, always used for shots on the forehand side, means turning the hand slightly to the right of the handle when the racket is held parallel to the ground and with the stringed face vertical. Your grip should be firm so the racket cannot twist in your hand.
2 To begin the shot you can take the racket straight back in line with the on-coming ball (as Chrissie does) or round in a loop past your face and down into the position shown in the picture. Your body should at this point be turned sideways with your weight on your back foot.
3 As you start your swing towards the ball, transfer your balance on to your leading foot so that your hips can swivel round with your body weight just as impact is made with the ball. This will give added pace to the shot. The point of impact should be slightly in front and right of you.
4 Allow the swing to complete its total follow-through.

Jimmy Connors
Flat, attacking forehand

Spare a thought for the fellow on the other side of the net as Jimmy Connors shapes up to play one of his favourite shots. It is obvious that he is enjoying the challenge of this rally and is absolutely relishing the thought of powering his strength behind yet another mighty forehand.

Jimmy likes to play at speed and tends to build up pace on each shot in an effort to leave his opponent floundering and vulnerable. His game is all or nothing. Everything is hit low and hard, without compromise, and therefore his margin for error over the net is very small. This can be a dangerous way of playing because, with such flat shots, if his timing is fractionally off he can lose control of the ball.

WHEN TO PLAY
This flat forehand is an attacking shot and should be used to generate pace and keep the pressure on your opponent in a rally. It should be hit into a gap, forcing him to move quickly. The object is to rush your opponent into making a weaker return with the ball dropping mid-court, allowing you to either approach the net or hit a winner.

HOW TO PLAY
1 The correct height to hit the ball for a flat forehand is between hip and waist level where it is most comfortable. The impact of racket on ball should take place slightly in front of the body.
2 The racket head simply swings straight through the ball with the wrist staying very firm to the end of the follow-through. It is an uncompromising shot, carrying speed but no spin.

Virginia Wade
Stretching, defensive forehand

Virginia Wade is really under pressure here! It will take all her ingenuity to work her way out of this situation. However, she has certainly not given up and her mind has switched into defensive gear.

Look at the firmness of her wrist. There has been very little backswing on this shot. She has asked her legs for maximum effort and her natural fitness has responded. She has even managed to keep her head still, giving her arm and racket every chance of smoothly completing a very difficult shot.

This type of fast-action situation shows Virginia at her best. Her instinct for survival is very strong and her ability to adapt her shots to fit each particular position proves her exciting talent. No wonder she is so beloved of tennis enthusiasts throughout the world.

COMMON FAULTS
1 Giving up trying to reach the ball.
2 Lacking confidence that you can efficiently get the ball back over the net.

WHEN TO PLAY
A stretching forehand will obviously be demanded whenever you are caught too far from the ball. On no account should you ever give up trying to reach a ball, no matter how distant it seems. It is amazing how many points are won with 'impossible' shots from stretching positions. Your confidence receives such a boost if you can bring about a spectacular unexpected winner.

HOW TO PLAY
1 Keep the stroke as short as possible with all your effort placed on the forward movement. Try not to jerk any part of your body.
2 The urgency of the shot will probably mean that your feet are not perfectly placed, but instinct will help you make the most of a split-second decision and you may well be amazed by your automatic reaction!.

Boris Becker
Passing forehand

Although Boris Becker has obviously been made to work hard for this shot, he seems to have everything under control for an attempted passing shot. We may assume his opponent has hit a forcing approach shot down the line and has moved to the net, looking for an easy placement volley to the other side of the court. He reckons without the grit of the young German!

Becker has a very flexible wrist and has used topspin to control this forehand pass as much as possible. Another advantage of topspin is that Becker can keep his opponent guessing as to whether he is going down the line or cross-court, as his wrist will only flick through at the last moment to set the direction. His face does not show any concern over this difficult shot — his quick footwork seems to have taken him into the correct position and his body is well-balanced.

WHEN TO PLAY
This is an 'all or nothing' shot. You are obliged to go all out for a winner here as you are out of position and your opponent has total command of the net, looking to hit a winning volley.

HOW TO PLAY
1 This is where pretty nifty footwork can come to your rescue. If you can move fast enough to reach the ball in time to make a properly controlled shot, a winner is possible.

2 Prepare your shot as you move to the ball, keeping your backswing short so that all your effort goes into forcing the ball back low and fast. Topspin will give you control and the element of deception as with flexibility of wrist the racket head can be whipped through at the last moment to shoot the ball cross-court rather than down the line.
3 Do not lift your head in an attempt to 'help' the ball over the net. Any jerkiness will result in loss of control.

Jimmy Connors
Fighting forehand

How else would we expect to see Jimmy Connors other than with hair flying in all directions and the fire of battle in his eyes! He could be in trouble on this shot, having been rushed into making it. However, he has still managed to get his leading foot planted, to give him stability and allow him to bring his weight forward.

His left foot is in the correct position waiting for the message to push his body back towards the centre of the baseline in readiness for the next shot.

Jimmy uses his body well. He always turns his shoulder to the net, which gives him free movement to play the shot with maximum power from his body. Being rushed, he would have cut down his backswing so that he was not late into the shot, but has still made sure of his follow-through to gain complete control of a difficult ball.

WHEN TO PLAY
You are in trouble. Your opponent is in full command of the rally and you are being rushed into making your shots. This where instinct and your ability to improvise come into play.

Because you have so little time, your mind is working overtime and your reactions will be quicker. Your feet have to work faster to get into a makeshift position that enables you to make the best of a difficult shot. Concentration and determination are vital.

HOW TO PLAY
1 Shorten your takeback to make sure the racket head meets the ball in front of you. Your feet and body should form a solid position so that you can use your weight to advantage.
2 Balance yourself and keep your body bending forwards as much as possible to obtain maximum control. If you fall backwards the ball will tend to rise.

Annabel Croft

Forehand winner

How fortunate Annabel Croft is! She possesses one of the most natural, uninhibited, winning forehands in the game today. She is happiest when bouncing round the balls approaching on her backhand to thump forehands all round the court. As in this picture she likes to take the mid-court shot on the rise to blast the ball out of reach of her opponent.

She is taking this ball very early and the object of this tactic is twofold. Firstly, it means that the ball will be back in her opponent's court quicker than expected. Secondly, because this shot will be hit for a winner, the trajectory of the ball will be downwards and therefore the higher (earlier) she takes the ball, the easier it will be to clear the net.

What this photograph does not show is the strong pivot of her hips as she hits the ball. That is where a lot of her power comes from. Her concentration and determination are obvious for all to see, but remember when you go for a winner that the rally is never won until the ball is dead.

COMMON FAULTS
1 Letting the ball drop too low. It is much more difficult to hit a winning forehand from below the height of the net.
2 Having your body too 'open' to the net. This loses not only pace but also control.

WHEN TO PLAY
A winning forehand should only be attempted when you can move forward easily on to a short ball carrying mid-pace. The racket head should make contact before the ball reaches its highest point. It can be hit either with topspin or slice.

HOW TO PLAY
1 Shorten your backswing as you move forward and get the racket head into line with the on-coming ball. Make sure you approach the ball at the correct angle to hit your winner into the chosen gap.
2 Lean on the ball with all your weight. Remember to give your racket enough room to sweep through uninhibited.

Pam Shriver

Sliced forehand

Surprisingly, Pam Shriver quite often finds herself in this position on her forehand, with the ball too close to her body. She has found an effective antidote to this problem by developing her own style of sliced forehand. The situation is likely to arise when she is returning serve, but she deals with it coolly and keeps control of her return. Her height – 6ft (1.8m) – is a great asset as the higher she takes the ball, the safer and more effective the slice will be. Safe, because it reaches the net at a higher point and effective, because it 'digs' into the court at a sharper angle.

However it must be observed that this habit of asking her body to assume unnatural positions may well have contributed to the fact that rarely is she seen off-court without ice packs on her arm and shoulder 'as a precautionary measure'. Do note that you must be aware of your body as it gives out warning signals. If your arm, especially the elbow or shoulder, develops any aches or pains you should seek medical advice immediately, but also have your game analysed to see if a particular shot is aggravating the situation.

COMMON FAULTS
1 Opening the face of the racket too much, causing the ball to lift out over the baseline.
2 Not completing the follow-through, negating the effect of the slice.

HOW TO PLAY
1 Putting slice on the forehand means the racket has to cut down the back of the ball at a diagonal angle with the face of the racket slightly open. Therefore the racket head must start its forward swing higher than the flight of the on-coming ball.

2 Slice put on over the whole stroke will keep control of the ball in a rally. A heavier slice is more effective, especially on a clay or grass court, as the ball will barely rise off the ground and your opponent will be obliged to lift the return, giving you the opportunity to attack.

Anders Jarryd

Flat backhand

This cannot be mistaken for anything other than a flat backhand. Look how the whole racket is held parallel to the ground, firmly supported by the solidity of the two-handed grip. Note also the bounce in Anders Jarryd's feet — how about that for being on your toes!

Also notice that he is looking over his right shoulder as he watches the ball. That tells you that he has turned sideways to get as much body weight as possible behind the shot. His right arm is fully extended showing that he is not cramped in his position.

Jarryd has already transferred his weight on to his leading foot and the racket head has started its straight path to hit through the ball. From the position of his body, it would appear that he is going to sweep this ball cross-court. If he had been going down the line his right foot would have been slightly further over to give him the correct angle.

COMMON FAULTS
1 Dropping the head of the racket, caused by weak wrist action.
2 Starting your preparation too late. You cannot make up lost time.

WHEN TO PLAY
This is a classic, unhurried shot, played from the baseline during a rally. It is a useful stroke as the ball should carry deep to the other side of the court keeping your opponent pinned on the baseline. Nowadays, however, fewer players tend to play flat groundstrokes because total control can be difficult, preferring the security of a shot carrying slice or topspin.

HOW TO PLAY
1 To play a flat backhand, take the racket either straight back or in a loop up past the side of your head so that the shaft reaches a point parallel with the ground. Between hip and waist is the ideal track the racket should follow when coming forward for a straight hit through the ball. The grip for shots on the backhand is the Western. With the racket parallel to the ground but the stringed face vertical, turn your grip slightly to the left on the racket handle.
2 In the two-handed shot, both hands are on the grip during the takeback and follow-through. For a one-handed backhand, the support hand should assume a hold nearer the throat of the racket to help guide the racket head into the correct position. This hand should simply let go as the racket starts its forward movement and should then be used as an aid to balance.

Carling Bassett
Two-handed backhand

The advent of the two-handed backhand has made the learning of this more difficult groundstroke considerably easier — in fact many coaches now prefer to teach the two-handed shot to youngsters coming in to the game. Carling Bassett is a flamboyant character and there is nothing she likes better than producing gasps of admiration from the spectators as she lets fly her two-hander.

This picture shows how useful two hands can be in getting you out of a difficult spot — she has obviously been too close to the ball and therefore cramped in her stroke, but has gained extra power using her left arm to push the racket arm forward.

Carling's face shows her effort but the game of tennis is never perfect and part and parcel of the sport is the ability to combat difficult positions. It must be said, however, that playing with two hands on the backhand requires excellent anticipation and footwork as the length of stretch is severely restricted.

COMMON FAULTS
1 Getting too close to the ball.
2 Not completing the follow-through.

WHEN TO PLAY
It is essential that consistency is achieved so that you have confidence in playing this shot time and time again. The two-handed backhand will come into its own in baseline rallies. Most two-handers are seemingly invincible from the back of the court. The second hand certainly adds solidity and a certain amount of deception can be gained by fractional changes in the angle of the racket head, made easier by having two hands on the racket.

HOW TO PLAY
1 The supporting hand is placed as close to the leading hand as is comfortable, with the palm of the hand solidly behind the racket handle. This hand's job is to give added pushing power to the racket. It is, in fact, the more important hand as the leading wrist is notably weak and unreliable on the backhand side.
2 Make a straight or looped takeback, as explained for the flat backhand and bring the racket forward to hit the ball between waist and hip level.
3 Make sure you allow the racket to complete the follow-through.

COMMON FAULTS
1 Not completing the follow-through, producing a shot that flies over the baseline.
2 Dropping the racket head to reach the low ball instead of bending the knees, producing a scooped shot.

WHEN TO PLAY
The backhand slice is a patient shot. It is played when you are vying with your opponent about who is going to take the initiative in a rally. From the baseline it is a safety shot during a rally, but it can also be played from a defensive situation. If you play it from the baseline, the slice gives the ball sufficient 'lift' to ensure that it clears the net. It will also 'dig' into the court (especially clay or grass) and keep the ball very low. On concrete the ball will come through low and fast.

Virginia Wade
Sliced backhand

What a classic backhand slice this is. With eyes fixed firmly on the ball and total determination written all over her face, Virginia Wade's preparation for this shot is perfect.

The ball is obviously coming in low and, while positioning her right foot for balance, Virginia has automatically bent her knees to allow her racket head to come in at the right angle. The racket face is already 'open' (tilted slightly backwards) to put a slice under the ball which will lift it over the net.

This particular shot is not forced. It is played deliberately with complete control, probably looking for depth. She is quite content to play it simply to continue the rally, waiting for the right opportunity to attack.

HOW TO PLAY

1 The backhand grip, whether you are hitting flat, topspin or slice, is slightly to the left of the central position on the handle (Western grip). The thumb position is very important as it must spread slightly across the back of the racket to give solidity. The three basic grips for tennis shots — Eastern (forehand), Western (backhand) and 'chopper' (serve), should all be as close to each other as possible to facilitate easy movement of the hand on the racket grip.

2 For a sliced backhand, the left hand should help to support the racket head in the takeback. This will encourage the body to turn sideways. The racket head starts its swing at a higher point than the oncoming ball and continues through a diagonal movement, gradually coming down the back of the ball. The racket head should meet the ball in front of your body and your weight should be on your leading foot. The follow-through continues to the full extent of your arm to keep maximum control.

Gabriela Sabatini
Topspin backhand

Gabriela Sabatini has a wonderful natural flair for hitting topspin and this stroke is totally uninhibited. Topspin requires a supple wrist as its flexibility will determine the amount of spin you put on the ball.

You can see the angle of the racket head as it begins its forward and upward flight. Her left hand has finished its supporting role, having helped guide and support the racket head into the correct position for the swing. It will now help as an aid to balance.

Gabriela's weight has moved on to her leading foot, her body is sideways to the net and her face is full of purpose and conviction. It looks as though this shot cannot fail.

Imagine the continuation of the stroke in the complete follow-through. The arc of the racket goes from low to high on a diagonal angle and the swing carries on to its fullest extent. The wrist turns over during this long stroke to create the topspin on the ball. The shot should then clear the net with a good margin for error and bounce high on the opposite baseline.

COMMON FAULTS
1 Falling back on to your rear foot, producing an open (back-tilted) racket face. No topspin will be possible from this angle.
2 Not completing the follow-through.

WHEN TO PLAY
One of the most useful times to play topspin is in breaking up your opponent's rhythm during a rally. It is necessary to be aware of whether your opponent has settled into a groove and is happy to play at the pace you are setting. You should always keep your opponent guessing, and with topspin you can either slow the pace and make the ball bounce high or quicken it by making a low, controlled shot. The speed of the ball depends on how fast you bring your wrist over during the execution of a shot carrying topspin.

John McEnroe
Running backhand

One of the requisites for good tennis is fast, efficient footwork. Regardless of how accurate your shots are, if you cannot move easily towards the ball, your level of achievement will be limited. Being slim and fit helps, but if movement does not come naturally, hard training on short sprints will be required.

John McEnroe has always moved well about the court. Not only is he naturally light on his feet, but his anticipation of where his opponent's shot is going gives him a fraction of a second longer to get into position.

The need for rapid movement does not disrupt his concentration on the shot. On this running backhand he is perfectly balanced and his racket is already in position, just waiting to be brought forward to meet the ball. He makes it look simple, but there is a feeling of urgency about this shot which confirms that speed about the court is absolutely essential.

COMMON FAULTS
1 Slow footwork, giving you no chance to attempt a proper shot.
2 Over-running, making it impossible to get back into court for the next shot.

WHEN TO PLAY
Your opponent has taken control of the rally by working you out of position on the baseline. He has you scampering from the forehand corner to the backhand and preparation in mid-flight is paramount. The impetus of your movement will automatically help to bring your weight into the shot, but remember to be prepared to push back towards the centre of the baseline *after* you have played the shot to be ready for the next ball.

HOW TO PLAY
1 As with all shots played on the run, the backswing should be shortened so that you can control the racket head. Your non-racket hand gives vital support here.
2 Try to judge your pace so that you are balanced with your leading foot firmly placed as you come into hit the ball. This will ensure that your weight is directed into the ball, rather than being wasted by over-running a couple of paces.

John Lloyd

Stretching backhand

Here is where a one-handed backhand has benefits over a two-handed shot. Could John Lloyd find any further stretch in his body? So intent is he on running down the ball that his back is towards the net and he is relying on the image of the court in his mind's eye to give direction to his return. The only shot open to him in this position is a lob, as high and as deep as he can manage to give him time to recover.

There is no doubt that he is going to reach the ball and, although the situation looks desperate, at least he will make his opponent play another shot. There is always the chance that he might make an error through rushing or taking his eye off the ball.

The pity of it is that he is not playing this particular shot from the other side of the net! His lob would then have had the setting sun behind it (note the length of the shadows) making the smash more difficult for his opponent.

COMMON FAULTS
1 Not even attempting to reach the ball.
2 Attempting a 'flash' shot in the unrealistic hope of hitting a winner.

HOW TO PLAY
1 Hundred per cent effort is essential here. Basically you must tighten your grip on the racket, stretch to your fullest extent and meet the ball with a firm wrist.
2 As a backswing is not possible, the racket arm must be forced forwards with the face slightly open to make sure the ball goes upwards in a lob.
3 Do not pull back from the stroke through fear of falling.

Ivan Lendl
Deceptive backhand

You can almost see Ivan Lendl's brain ticking over as he comes in to play this sliced backhand. But are we sure he will play a sliced shot? Could he not at the last moment drop his wrist and hit a rolling topspin backhand?

This is what tennis is all about — the ability to be aware of what your opponent is expecting, so you can take advantage by varying the shot. It keeps your opponent guessing, it keeps you in the driving seat. It also gives you a lot of satisfaction and there is nothing better than being one jump ahead in a match. But deep concentration also works wonders for keeping out extraneous noises — the click of the photographers' cameras, the unexpected cry of a child, the umpire's voice from the match on the next-door court.

If you find your mind wandering even to the point of knowing when a friend has come to watch, you must shake yourself into focusing only on the game. Work at winning the next point then the one after that, slowly building up until you are finally swallowed up in your own cocoon of concentration. Unless you are immersed in your own and your opponent's actions, you may not recognize the perfect moment to play a deceptive shot.

COMMON FAULTS
1 Changing your mind several times before trying to hit the ball.
2 Signalling your intention to your opponent by preparing the shot too early.

WHEN TO PLAY
Deceptive shots can be played when you have enough time to change your mind. There is a world of difference between changing your mind intentionally and simply not knowing which shot to play. If the deception is played really cleverly and intuitively, your opponent's anticipation of your game will become totally confused.

HOW TO PLAY
1 Timing is all. The angle of the racket head must be changed only at the last moment, so your opponent is not aware of it until too late.
2 Make sure you are definite in your own mind so that you play your chosen shot completely. Otherwise you will end up with an amalgam of different shots and fail miserably in your idea.

Boris Becker
Defensive backhand

How hot and strained Boris Becker appears to be as he struggles to remain in this point. More than likely he is in the middle of a long, close match where every point is vital and his opponent is on the offensive.

This is the moment when concentration and conviction can be lost and you suddenly find yourself struggling for existence. Your head feels as though it is bursting, the court surroundings seem unreal and the match is slipping away too quickly.

The way to combat this pressure is to slow down between points, take your full 30 seconds, and allow your breathing to return to normal. Flex arm and leg muscles to help them relax and generally work towards clearing your mind for the task in hand. Nobody enjoys being strained on every shot and it is only by cool evaluation of this situation that the light at the end of the tunnel may be seen.

COMMON FAULTS
1 Not bending to the ball, putting unrealistic reliance on the arm only to control the shot.
2 Fear of falling over. This makes the body rigid.

WHEN TO PLAY
Defensive groundstrokes play a vital part in any match. It stands to reason that you cannot always be in total command, unless your opponent is very much weaker than yourself. To fight your way out of a stranglehold demands determination, but to be a winner you must be able to meet every challenge.

There is no conventional way out of trouble — every player responds individually to a crisis — but every winner has one thing in common, the refusal to believe that he or she is beaten.

HOW TO PLAY
1 Bend your knees to get into position for this low shot. The backswing will have to be shortened as time is limited. Keep your wrist firm so that the racket can meet the ball positively.
2 Try to stay as relaxed as possible. The bend of your body will help your control. The type of return open to you in this situation is a looped shot or a lob, giving you time to recover.

Kathy Jordan

Serve – ready position

This is the moment to collect your thoughts on where you are about to hit your serve. Kathy Jordan is not just aiming to get her serve into the correct, diagonally opposite service box. She will be weighing up whether the ball should fall down the middle line, wide to the sidelines or in a straight line with the body of her opponent.

For example, if she is playing a left-hander, she may wish to play a slice serve to pull her opponent out wide on the backhand. By following such a serve into the net, the chances are that she could then punch the resulting volley cross-court into the opposite corner.

If the score stands at 30-all, she may decide to hit a fast serve down the middle to cut the angle on the return. If she is in the unenviable position of being 0-40 down and about to hit a second serve, her thoughts are probably geared to getting in a deep second serve to stop her opponent from chipping the return and moving to the net to take command.

There should always be thoughts and ideas in your head about the correct tactics on each point. That way nerves play no part.

HOW TO PLAY

1 The ready position is very individual. The main stipulation is that both your feet should start *behind* the line. A foot on the line is a footfault. Behind the baseline means standing with your leading foot up to the line.

2 For singles you should stand behind the baseline close to the centre line, so that you can cover the return equally well to either side of the court.

3 For doubles you can stand anywhere behind the baseline between the centre line and the outside side-line, but somewhere in the middle of that area is the normally accepted position. However, many difficult angles can be achieved from wide stances and your opponent has then the problem of working out where to stand in order to receive the serve.

Hana Mandlikova

Serve – throw up

If only we could all have such an elegant and effective serve as Hana Mandlikova.

One of the most difficult parts of the serve is achieving consistency in the throw-up of the ball. Unless it can be placed time and time again in the same place and at the same height, confidence in serving will be slow in coming.

Practise placing the ball in the air without attempting to hit it and note where it bounces. It should fall slightly in front and to the right of you if you are right-handed, or to the left if you are left-handed. Hana has placed the ball beautifully and her body is turned sideways waiting for the throw of the racket head. The ball must be tossed high enough to allow you to complete the build-up to your serve and make impact at your fullest stretch.

COMMON FAULTS
1 Attempting to hit a badly placed ball. Rather abandon it without trying to strike it, and start your whole service action again.
2 Throwing the ball too low, forcing yourself into making a cramped serve.

Ivan Lendl

Service action

What an ideal teaching photograph this is! Ivan Lendl not only demonstrates the correct position and balance for his serve, but also imparts to us the power about to be unleashed on the ball.

The ball may appear to have been thrown too high, but if you work this shot through you will realize that by the time Lendl achieves his full stretch, the racket head will meet the ball as it has reached its maximum height and begins to drop. This is the perfect hitting point.

He is still sideways to the net at this moment and his body will whip into the serve only as contact with the ball is being made. The force then exerted behind the ball will be without compromise and it is not surprising that Lendl has been known to serve out a game with four untouchable aces.

His right foot comes forward only once the ball has been struck, to help him regain balance.

WHEN TO PLAY

This is a full-blooded first serve, hit flat. Your full power should be used when you are totally confident that a high percentage of first serves will be successful. If you do not have this confidence, reduce the speed to 75 per cent to gain more consistency.

HOW TO PLAY

1 The grip is the 'chopper' — pick up the racket as you would a hammer and grip it firmly. Stand with your feet at a comfortable distance apart, sideways to the net and in a position *behind* the baseline so that neither foot touches the line.
2 The arc of the swing is very individual and there are no hard-and-fast rules, other than that the racket head should eventually assume a throwing position behind your head and down your back. An easy way to achieve this action is to stand in front of a full length mirror and pretend to throw a ball overhand. This shows you the movement of the wrist as it snaps through at point of flight and gives you the feel of the shot.
3 Throw the ball high and accurately placed (see previous page).
4 The body should remain sideways until point of impact, when the full weight of its turn will add power to the hit. The legs play a vital part in balance and as the pushing-off point for the full stretch towards the ball.

John McEnroe
Leaning into the serve

This remarkable picture captures a split-second action: the shutter snapped just at the right moment to hold in suspension the wonderful angle John McEnroe achieves on his serve as his weight complements the throwing action of his racket. There is no opting out on this one. He has committed himself to powering a heavy serve into court and following it into the net.

Think how far this 'lean' will help him on his way up the court. In fact his feet have already left the ground as they jump up towards the ball and forwards into court. It is legal to jump as long as your feet do not touch the baseline or the inside of the court *before* you have hit the ball.

Can you imagine being on the receiving end of a serve that looks so totally powerful? It is a daunting prospect. Therefore, it should really be your aim to achieve a correctly produced and athletic serve, even though you will hit the ball less strongly than McEnroe. A good service action can confound your opponent into believing that such a well-practised shot must carry speed.

COMMON FAULTS
1 Not throwing far enough ahead to allow the lean.
2 Throwing the ball too far ahead causing the racket head to meet it at the wrong angle. Rather let the ball drop and start your service action again.

HOW TO PLAY
If you have followed this section through the previous three pictures, you will realize how the 'lean' plays its part in the make-up of the serve. If the throw-up is in front of you and the ball is high enough, the lean and the full stretch will fall naturally into place.

There is nothing more rewarding than working through the facets of the serve until you can hit the ball with such timing that it zings off the racket at a speed which amazes even you! Practice is everything on the serve — each part of the action should be learned and all are equal in their importance to the full effect.

Gabriela Sabatini

Serve – follow through

To finish this section on the first serve it is necessary to look at the follow-through. It is so easy to forget its importance. Gabriela Sabatini gives the impression of having gone for a big first serve here with her weight still coming forward and her hair flying out with the speed and effort of the shot.

Her racket head has carried on after impact, completing the powerful follow-through that allows her to gain total control of the flight of the ball. Her body weight has come in fully behind the ball and she is now perfectly placed facing forwards. Her right foot is just starting to come through and this will form the first step towards following her serve into the net.

If she were to decide to play out the rally from the back of the court instead of approaching the net, she would just pull back on to her right foot and find herself in the correct position behind the baseline.

COMMON FAULTS
1 Do not be in a hurry to stop the flowing action of the follow-through in an attempt to assume readiness for the next shot.
2 Make certain that the racket head finishes diagonally across your body rather than straight down the side.

Kevin Curren v Boris Becker
Second serve

The most speculative part of the game of tennis is how and when the serve will be broken. Even nowadays with the advent of the tiebreak, the break of serve is still one of the most exciting parts of a match.

It takes courage and opportunism to face, and return positively, a ball that can be approaching you at over 100 miles (160km) per hour. So what you really have to seize on is the chance your opponent gives you when he misses his big first serve, as the second serve tends to be more vulnerable — or at least playable.

This is the opportunity Boris Becker has taken as Kevin Curren shapes up for his second serve. Becker has automatically moved in a couple of paces. This tells his opponent that he is not afraid of the second serve and that he is expecting to attack it. It is pure intimidation of course, but totally legitimate, and it is amazing how many times a weak serve is delivered or, at worst, a double fault is presented.

Psychologically Curren is at a disadvantage here. He knows Becker will try to take command, so his survival instinct will tell him to hit a deep second serve which can pin Becker back on the baseline. Otherwise he could go for an angle (with a wide slice, for example), to catch his opponent unawares. He must be safe but bold. As he prepares to serve he will take a few deep breaths, refusing to be hurried. He will decide in his own mind which tactics to pursue. And, for sure, he will be promising himself not to fault on his next first serve!

COMMON FAULTS
1 *When serving*
● Rushing into your serve, causing weakness and possibly a double fault.
● Not thinking out your best move.

2 *When receiving*
● Receiving the second serve from the same ready position as the first. Move in and threaten it.
● Not being prepared to take a chance on the return, especially on break point.

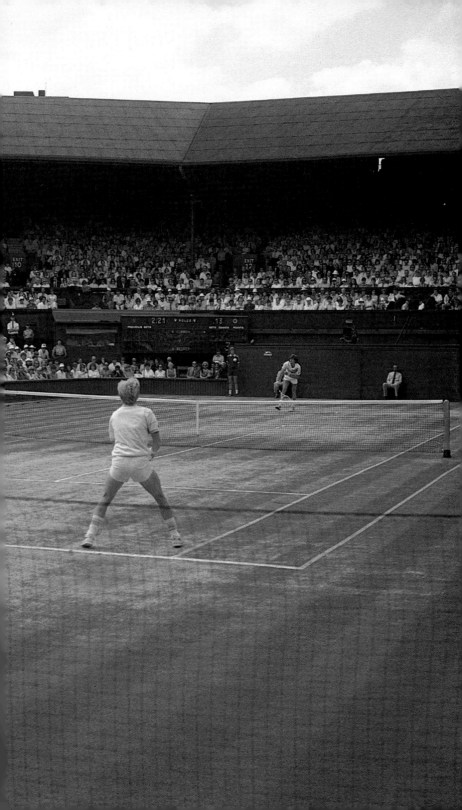

Anders Jarryd
Return of serve

There are some serious thoughts going through Anders Jarryd's head as he waits to return serve. It is vital that you have some form of plan in your head at the start of each point as a poor return of serve offers continuing advantage to the server.

To combat a serve-and-volleyer
● Try blocking the return, keeping the ball low over the net and dropping it at your opponent's feet, forcing him to hit upwards. Blocking a return means hitting the ball without a backswing, combining your own impact with the speed already on the ball.
● Move back a couple of paces to give yourself more time to see the ball and judge its pace.
● If you are in real trouble, lob the return. This will certainly take your opponent by surprise and probably catch him wrong-footed.

To combat a wide serve
● As your opponent begins his serve, start moving out towards the sideline. You will then be in a better position to hit a positive return off a wide serve. Do remember, though, that by moving early, you lay yourself open to an ace down the middle line.
● Try moving in to take the ball earlier, thereby cutting the angle.

COMMON FAULTS
1 Standing upright with the racket placed across your body.
2 Positioning yourself in one particular place to cover your weaker side.

HOW TO PLAY
1 You should be full of alert anticipation when you are in the ready position to receive serve. After all, you have but a split second to see how the ball is coming through.

2 You should be on your toes with your knees bent, ready to spring into action. The racket head should be in a central position in front of you making a forehand or a backhand equally easy to assume.

Martina Navratilova

Forehand volley

This picture of Martina Navratilova hitting a forehand volley speaks for itself. Perfection on a tennis court is rarely seen, but this comes pretty close to the ideal.

Martina makes volleying look easy and that is exactly what it is to her! She works the rally so well that by the time she comes to hit a volley, it is simply the icing on the top of the cake. This is beauty of most top players — it is the spadework done beforehand that actually makes it easy to bring out the spectacular shot. However, Martina knows the point is not won until the ball is out of her opponent's reach, so her eyes are riveted on the ball making sure she plays the shot positively.

Volleying is exciting. It requires quick eye and arm reactions. It demands alertness and athletic agility. All tennis players should learn the net position. There is nothing more satisfying than finishing off a well-fought rally with a winning volley.

COMMON FAULTS
1 Not being close enough to the net when volleying.
2 Allowing the wrist to slacken.

WHEN TO PLAY
This particular forehand volley is unhurried. The ball has come in exactly where expected and Martina has all the time in the world to decide where to hit it. It could be the follow up to a first serve where she is looking for a winning placement volley. Or it may be part of a rally in which she has waited for the correct shot on which to approach and has found herself in complete command of the net. This one is in the bag!

HOW TO PLAY
1 Because it is a reaction shot, the volley must necessarily be kept to a very short stroke. There should be no floppy backswing. Rather the wrist should be so firm that the head of the racket remains constantly in line with the ball. The ball should be struck at a point slightly in front of the body.
2 The volley is a short punching movement with no follow-through. This risks your racket hitting the net, which loses you the point.
3 Make sure you give your racket arm enough room, as a cramped volley is a bad volley. Your weight should be coming forward to add pace.

Pam Shriver
High forehand volley

Being tall may not be ideal for fast movement around the court, but for high volleys it is definitely an advantage! Pam Shriver is not only tall, she is strong and it is the strength in her wrist, upper arm and shoulder that allows her to play high volleys with such confidence and effectiveness.

High volleys give problems to most people when learning because the wrist tends not to be firm enough, allowing the racket head to waver. This makes meeting the ball in the correct place somewhat of a lottery. Judging the height of a ball is difficult, too.

In this shot, Pam's wrist is firm, the racket head is in line with the ball and her shoulder is giving solid back-up. With the racket head so far in front of her, it looks as if she is about to play an angled cross-court volley.

COMMON FAULTS
1 'Flapping' at the ball, making control impossible.
2 Letting the ball drop and then hitting it with a bent elbow.

WHEN TO PLAY
The easiest high volley comes as you approach the net after a good serve and the return is defensively lifted. With your weight coming into this shot, you would be looking to hit an outright winner of this ball.

A more difficult task is moving in to meet and volley a looped ball aimed to the baseline. This means you will take it early (above head height), to give sufficient clearance over the net and depth on the other side of the court. This allows you to get closer to the net for the next volley, which may then be a winner.

HOW TO PLAY
1 The wrist must be firm so that you are aware of the position of the racket head. There is no takeback, other than getting the racket into the hitting position by the shortest possible route.
2 The shot is a forward punch of the racket head, with the racket immediately resuming its ready position after the hit in anticipation of the next ball.

Ivan Lendl
Half–volley

There are times when even the best are caught with the ball at their feet and compensating action must be taken. Ivan Lendl has had to put the brakes on, halting his forward charge to the net, as he deals with a return that has caught him mid-court. Even with his feet together he is well-balanced and his attitude indicates that after he has dealt with this spot of trouble, he will continue his forward route.

A half-volley is a delicate shot played with touch. Timing is essential as the ball is hit *immediately* after the bounce. By adjusting the racket head, sharp angles can be achieved and, because the ball is taken early, your opponent may be surprised at the speed of its return.

However, a half-volley can also be a defensive shot because you have been caught in completely the wrong position. This means that the best you can do will be to lift the ball in a scoop carrying very little pace and, because you are in a bad position, the chances are that your opponent will be one point better off.

COMMON FAULTS
1 Lifting your head as you play the ball, to see where it is going. This jerks the ball out of control.
2 Getting tied up in knots and losing your balance when the ball falls right beside your feet.

WHEN TO PLAY
If your tactics are to attack, then it will follow that your opponent will move to stop your onslaught and may attempt this by chipping returns low over the net, judging them finely to fall at your feet. You cannot volley them as they are too low and you cannot stop your forward movement in time to hit a drive — the half-volley is a compromise.

The only way to combat this tactic is to move faster into the front court and take the low return on the volley, or hold back just inside the baseline to give yourself time to play a proper approach shot.

HOW TO PLAY
1 Instinct will warn you to get the racket head into position as quickly as possible, so cut your backswing.
2 The wrist should be firm to play your chosen angle and the knees must be bent to allow the ball to be played from the correct position.
3 In order to keep control of the ball, you may need to add topspin. This will help the ball up and over the net quickly, with the spin dipping the ball into court on the other side.

Pam Shriver
Low backhand volley

When split-second timing is necessary, it is amazing how often the eyes are not watching the ball. Nevertheless Pam Shriver is about to hit a classic low backhand volley and she will never know that at the moment of impact she was working on automatic pilot!

But just look at her. The picture shows controlled aggression. Pam dislikes baseline rallies, preferring to trust her luck at the net to her quick reactions and natural instincts. Her temperament responds better to immediacy. The more time she has to play a shot the more hesitation there is in her thoughts.

So Pam will always push forwards aware that her volleying is reliable and devastating. A natural volleyer is like a Jack-in-the-Box — willing to bounce, bend and stretch as demanded by the position of the ball.

COMMON FAULTS
1 Dropping your wrist, producing a scooped shot.
2 Sticking out your racket half-heartedly, without conviction, hoping that it might hit the ball.

WHEN TO PLAY
A low backhand should be a routine part of your volley repertoire. You will be asked to play this shot both from mid-court and close in to the net.

Try to take the ball before it drops too low — a low attacking volley can very quickly turn into a difficult, defensive 'dig' as you try to pick the ball off your toes.

HOW TO PLAY
1 Keep your wrist firm and bend your knees as necessary, as Pam is doing, bringing the racket head forward to meet the ball in front of your body. It will be a poor volley if you drop your wrist and scoop at the ball, rather than bend your knees to get into position.
2 Keep the face of the racket open, so that the ball will be helped upwards to clear the net.
3 Bring your weight forward and use your free arm to aid balance.

John McEnroe

High backhand volley

Look at the urgency on the face of John McEnroe as he hits this backhand volley. There is no doubt in his mind that he is in total control of this particular rally and he intends this volley to be a winner.

He is positioned slightly sideways to the ball, making sure he has enough room for the racket head to meet the ball solidly in front of his body. His weight is going forward, giving added power and control to the shot.

From the position of his right hand, you can see how short the stroke has been, thereby keeping complete control of the racket head.

WHEN TO PLAY

A winning backhand volley is the reward for playing positively and coolly.

There are two ways of getting to an attacking position at the net. The first is to move in behind a fast, well-placed serve, looking for a defensive return. The second is to work your opponent around the court so much that, unable to cope with the pressure, he drops the ball mid-court, enabling you to move into the net to hit the winning volley.

HOW TO PLAY

1 Imagine you have picked up a hammer. The grip you have assumed on the handle is basically the volley grip. The central position on top of the racket means that reaction can be swift to either forehand or backhand volley, regardless of how fast or unexpected the on-coming ball. There should be very little movement of the hand from the central grip, but a better backhand volley is produced by sliding the thumb along the back of the racket, giving more stability of grip.

2 The volley is a short, sharp stroke. The takeback of the racket head should go no further than the side of your head. This is because the ball is so quickly upon you that you must be able to react fast. If you take the racket back too far, you will be late into the volley.

3 Keep the wrist firm so that you meet the ball in total command of the racket head. The actual stroke should hit through the ball positively, but there is very little follow-through for two reasons:
● you could hit the net and therefore lose the point.
● you have to be prepared in case the ball comes back, so you should assume your central ready position as soon as possible.

Jimmy Connors
Two–handed volley

This shows the cheekiness of Jimmy Connors'
game! Although he seems to be hitting a
defensive volley off a ball that has been hit
almost straight at him, he has still managed to
turn things to his advantage and produce a
sharp and probably winning angle.

This is where two hands can be useful in a
volley. The extra hand gives double the firmness
and Jimmy has simply blocked the return with
his solid grip, angled the racket head and
literally used the speed off his opponent's ball
to hit his winner.

Jimmy enjoys confrontation. To him a tennis
match should be crammed full of incident and
the more tricky the situation, the better he
responds. He needs to be excited and it is this
heightened sensibility which allows him to
move up a gear and react positively to
threatening danger.

If you can make a winner of a defensive volley
of this kind, you should regard it as a 'gift'. It is
these lucky winners that add piquancy to a
tension-filled match.

COMMON FAULTS
1 Ducking away from
the ball, completely
giving up trying to hit
it.
2 Jerking the racket
head at the ball in an
attempt to push the
ball over the net.

WHEN TO PLAY
Although you are at the net, the
advantage is actually with your
opponent in this situation. He is
preparing to pass you, so your
defence is to read his mind and
position yourself to cut off his shot.
On these occasions it can happen
that, although you anticipate
correctly, you move into the path of
the ball and then have to defend not
only the point, but also your person.

HOW TO PLAY
1 The easiest way to take a ball
coming at your tummy is off the
backhand. It is a natural movement
to draw the racket head across your
body. If you attempted it off the
forehand side, you would find yourself
totally cramped.
2 Try to plant your feet firmly, to give
you extra stability.

Pascale Paradis

Diving volley

One of the pleasures of watching a natural mover is the appearance of perfect balance, no matter how difficult the position. A natural mover is born and has reactions so spontaneous that it looks as though the body is just flowing towards the ball. That's what makes such a player so exciting to watch.

Pascale Paradis is naturally athletic. Her build is willowy and supple. Bending, stretching, weaving and ducking are what tennis means to her and the faster she is asked to play, the better.

She is determined not to give up on this ball and has either attempted a very low volley at a tantalizing angle, or has hit a backhand touch half-volley diagonally cross-court to combat a shot that has obviously tested her to her limits.

Having such a degree of talent allows this kind of improvisation and if she makes this one, it will be a real show-stopper!.

COMMON FAULTS
1 Being unable to turn quickly enough to reach a ball at such an angle.
2 Seeing the ball too late to be able to do anything about it.

WHEN TO PLAY
This is a difficult one. When your opponent hits a sharp angle you will have to change direction quickly. However, you must attempt to play a positive shot but, unless you can squeeze a winning angle, your opponent will take the point by hitting the next ball into an empty court.

HOW TO PLAY
1 The movement of the body must be supple so that you do not twist yourself unnaturally.
2 Your wrist must be flexible to allow the racket head to attempt probably one of the most difficult shots in the game.
3 Try to keep your balance and get the racket head low to the ball without scooping.

John Fitzgerald

Smash – ready position

John Fitzgerald has not managed to put away a winning volley but he has achieved the next best thing. By forcing his opponent into a defensive lob, he has a relatively easy smash.

He is well-prepared. By shuffling his feet, he has made certain that he is directly under the ball. His left arm helps him in this. It is used as a directional aid, tracking the flight and height of the ball. His weight at the moment is on his back foot, but as he starts his stretch upwards for the strike, he will transfer it forward to add power to his shot.

Most of all, look at the position of the racket head. It is hanging in suspension behind his head just as it would for a serve. In fact the smash is a cut-down version of the service action. It is shortened in the take-back so the racket head is positioned in time for the strike.

WHEN TO PLAY

Although you may appear to be in command of a rally, having worked your way up to the net, it is quite a normal occurrence to be sent backwards as your opponent lofts a desperate ball high in the air. This shot, the lob, is designed to catch you off balance, but with controlled and expert backward or sideways footwork, the smash can be one of the most spectacular shots in the game of tennis.

HOW TO PLAY

1 Good footwork is the priority here as without it, no matter how fine an action you have, the stroke will be scrappy. The side-slip step is one of the best ways into position, as you are already turned sideways.

2 Prepare as you move into position. The racket head should be taken straight back into the throwing position in readiness for the movement forward.

3 Your wrist should snap through at point of impact to make sure that the racket head is at the angle to hit the ball diagonally downwards.

4 Never take your eye off the ball — remember a gust of wind can play havoc with its direction. Judge its flight with the aid of your non-racket hand, which will also help your balance.

5 The legs play a vital part, too. Notice how the back leg is bent ready for the push forward and upward towards the ball. The object is to hit the ball at the highest point possible, to get a steep downward angle.

Mats Wilander
Finished smash

This could be the 'after' picture for the shot shown on the previous page, except that Mats Wilander has had a much more difficult smash to hit. In fact, the lob has been so deep that, realizing that his footwork is not going to get him there in time, Mats has had to take a leap to reach the ball.

This is the real test of a good 'smasher' whether he has judged his jump at the ball to perfection to coincide with the correct hitting point.

With his weight going backwards, it may appear to be impossible to hit the ball with any power. This is where the strength of the wrist, arm and shoulder comes into its own. The body will help, too, with the stretch upwards and as much forward curl as is possible.

Every sinew in his body will be pulled taut and he can go all out for a spectacular winner, knowing that because he will be landing on his back foot, fast recovery may be difficult.

COMMON FAULTS
1 Hitting the ball late, causing it to fly up in the air.
2 Inefficient backwards movement, causing loss of balance.

WHEN TO PLAY
Your opponent really has you on the hop here. You could decide to let this ball drop and take it off the ground, because it has been hit so high and deep, but that would put you on the defensive. If you are confident in your smash and your feet will work you into position, then have a go, as you want to regain the initiative. Tennis is a game of charge and counter-charge so you should always be aware of the various options open to you and their consequences.

HOW TO PLAY
1 Abandon caution to the wind and show how athletic you are on this smash. You cannot hold back, or the point is lost. Your backward (or sideways) movement must be fast, with compact strides to keep your balance.
2 The leap must be controlled and timed to reach the ball at full stretch.
3 As you make contact, try to give direction to the ball by turing your wrist. A smash can win the point just by being well placed. It does not have to carry speed if it is hit into an empty space.
4 On a difficult smash, the emphasis is on the control of the forward movement of the racket head and the complete follow-through.

Ivan Lendl

Topspin lob

The topspin lob must be one of the most effective shots in the book, as it can change a defensive position into a winning one simply and literally by the flick of a wrist. The shot has been reborn in the modern game, re-emerging with the wave of topspin talent that swept in with Bjorn Borg and has flowed onward with Lendl and Becker. It is now frequently used and all who play it have one thing in common — a wrist that is not only strong but is also flexible. The ability to whip the racket head up the back and over the top of the ball brings about a shot that can be totally unplayable.

It is an extremely difficult shot to master as the amount of time the ball spends on the strings is so minimal that timing has to be perfect. How many times have you seen a ball shoot awkwardly off the frame of a racket in the attempted execution of topspin? However, the advantages gleaned from hitting a lob in this way are extensive.

COMMON FAULTS
1 Not enough wrist whip to control the ball's flight. Without this, the ball will still be going upwards as it clears the far baseline!
2 Completely mistiming the ball, sending it in the wrong direction.

WHEN TO PLAY
Your options are many and varied, even if you are pinned on the baseline with your opponent at the net. As long as you can rely on your feet to get you into position in time, a passing shot, a dink (blocked shot angled just to clear the net) or a lob is possible.

The topspin lob is the real show-stopper because it catches your opponent off-balance and unawares, unable to see until the very last moment what is happening, because of the deception of the wrist. By the time he realizes, the ball is probably over his head and all he can do is watch and applaud.

HOW TO PLAY
1 Deception must be used here so prepare as you would for a normal shot then, at the last moment, drop your wrist so the racket falls below the height of the on-coming ball.
2 Whip the racket head up the back and over the top of the ball in a short, fast movement. This will pull the ball violently upward and the mighty spin will drop the ball speedily into court deep on the other side of the net.
3 Perfect timing will help to achieve accuracy.
4 Even should you mistime the ball, your opponent will still have problems hitting the smash as the ball will be wavering in the air.

Chris Evert Lloyd
Two-handed backhand lob

Chris Evert Lloyd is a cool customer. She knows exactly what she can and what she can't do on a tennis court. That's why you will very rarely see her attempt a 'flash' shot. Everything is calculated right down to the degree of accuracy she can expect from hitting this conventional two-handed backhand lob.

Chrissie bases her game on security. She likes to feel the ball on the strings of her racket for as long as she can, so her strokes are long and flowing. This way she knows she can control the direction and pace of her return.

Here she has been forced wide and with her two-handed grip she has simply tilted the face of the racket slightly backwards to meet the ball at the angle that will sent it upwards. Her grip is very firm. There is no doubt that this lob will be on its way smoothly to the chosen spot.

WHEN TO PLAY
Lots of youngsters will insist on trying to wallop their way out of trouble with heavy groundstrokes and all they succeed in doing is giving away the point. They seem to regard it as a sign of weakness to hoist the ball high and deep in an attempt to recover composure. But the lob shows awareness of danger and that you are intelligently working your way out of it.

A lob can also be used to break up the pace of a rally. You may feel that you are being unwillingly but inevitably swept along by the dictates of your opponent and your consistency is breaking down. Toss up a lob and the slower ball may well break the rhythm and throw your opponent off balance, so that you can take over control.

HOW TO PLAY
1 Grip the racket tightly and move the head into position in line with the ball. This lob will be hit flat.
2 Simply tilt the racket face back into the open position and play the ball solidly through an upward and forward swing. The angle of the racket head will dictate direction.
3 It is only by practice that you will achieve accuracy. A lob should be hit for height (to get it over your opponent's head), depth (to make your opponent scuttle from net to baseline) and direction (to put the ball out of reach).

Chris Evert Lloyd
The dropshot

This is the age of power in tennis. To achieve control and consistency while hitting the ball as hard as possible seems to be the overwhelming object of the exercise. But thank goodness for the individual who appreciates the finer points of the game!

Watch Chris Evert Lloyd's methodical dissection of her opponent's game. Just when the agony of defence becomes too great, she will put an end to the suffering by suddenly caressing a dropshot neatly over the net. It is a joy to watch the switch from aggressive pounding of groundstrokes to the light touch and accuracy of the dropshot. This versatility is one of the marks of a true talent.

Chris plays this shot with backspin that will curtail the forward movement of the ball when it bounces. The closer the dropshot falls on the other side of the net, the better. In fact it can happen that a ball will bounce back over the net if enough backspin is effected.

COMMON FAULTS
1 Not putting enough backspin on the ball, making the dropshot less effective.
2 Standing open to the net with your weight on your heels, prodding jerkily forwards at the ball.

WHEN TO PLAY
A dropshot should only be played when you are fully in command of a rally and your opponent has hit a mid-court ball. Because of the delicacy of the stroke, a dropshot should not be attempted from the baseline.

If you opponent likes to hug the back of the court, a dropshot should be used persistently. However, make sure that you maintain the element of surprise. Do be careful not to hit a dropshot when you are game point down. There is no need to take such a risk.

HOW TO PLAY
1 Approach the ball as if you are going to slice it. At the last moment cut heavily underneath the ball as if you are trying to slice it in half. This puts on the backspin.
2 There will only be enough forward movement on the ball to carry it a limited distance so do not play this shot from too far back.
3 A high percentage of touch and accuracy must be achieved, otherwise the ball will carry too far into your opponent's court, bringing it within easy reach.

Ivan Lendl

Backhand approach shot

Many tennis players play effectively along the baseline. The same players can play equally effectively from the net. Where their game falls apart is in the shot linking groundstrokes to volleys — the approach shot.

The major problem here is that this particular shot is hit on the run moving forwards. Another reason for weak approach shots is lack of practice. Think of your own training sessions. When you decide to hit a few volleys do you work your way up to the net during a rally, playing a groundstroke, an approach shot and then a volley? Or do you walk up to the net and assume a volleying position before starting a ball into play? The chances are that the second example applies.

Tennis is made up of continuous rallies. One shot leads into the next and all must be competently hit. Ivan Lendl's game flows naturally and for him playing an approach shot is just another link in the chain.

COMMON FAULTS
1 Rushing to the shot, stopping to hit the ball, then starting to move forwards again. All this is too jerky.
2 Not using your knees, dropping the head of the racket instead and producing a rising shot.

WHEN TO PLAY
An approach shot moves you from the baseline to the net. It is played when the ball falls mid-court and you wish to take advantage of its short length to pressurize your opponent. The most comfortable place to take such a shot is slightly lower than your waist, so you can use your body to lean into the shot for pace and control.

An effective spin on the backhand side is slice, as on a clay or grass court the ball will dig into the court and stay very low. Approach shots can be played down the line, cross-court, or even straight at your opponent deep on the baseline.

HOW TO PLAY
1 Choose a shot falling mid-court which you can comfortably move towards. Approach to the side of the ball, to give room to swing forward as you carry on towards the net.
2 Control the head of the racket with your supporting hand and slide the racket face down the back of and through the ball to effect the slice. Play it smoothly, aiming just over the net but deep or angled to the other side of the court.
3 Ensure that your knees are bent to allow the racket to come in at the right position.
4 Play the whole shot smoothly and continuously on the move.

Pat Cash

Low forehand approach

This shot is not of Pat Cash's choosing. His opponent has him on the run and has deliberately brought him forward. However little does he know that Pat is just about to turn the tables on him by hitting a controlled forehand approach, down the line from the way the face of the racket is pointing, and following it into the net.

He has only just made it though — look how low his racket is — but given that he has enough court area between him and the net, he will be able to hit the ball over without too much lift.

Adrenalin must be flowing here. Pat's senses will be so heightened, because he is working at speed, that the chances are that he will be in position for the volley almost before his opponent has hit the return. He cannot stop his forward impetus and with all his weight coming into the volley, it should be untouchable!.

WHEN TO PLAY
You are under pressure. The ball is low and short. You are coming from the back court and because you are running fast, you are committed to carrying on up to the net. It would be tennis suicide to try to halt your forward impetus after reaching this ball. All you would achieve would be a jerky movement of both body and racket resulting in total loss of control of the ball. Try changing defense into attack on this shot.

HOW TO PLAY
1 Your legs are all important here. They have to be quick enough to get you to the ball in time and they have to be flexible enough to maintain balance as you bend towards the ball.
2 Note how Pat is pretty open to the net as he stretches forward. There is no time for a backswing so you should keep your wrist firm as you reach for the ball and allow the momentum to push your body weight behind the ball, aiding both the shot and the continuing approach to net.

Yannick Noah

Forehand approach – timing

Yannick Noah is certainly in trouble here and forced to improvise. His problem offers a useful lesson in the importance of good timing on an approach shot. He must have been meaning to approach the net, but his opponent has obviously been one jump ahead and seems to have caught him completely out of position.

He is, however, in a perfectly acceptable position just outside the service area. Perhaps he changed his mind on the way in and decided to attempt a couple of extra paces to play a volley instead of the relative safety of an approach shot. Or perhaps he misjudged the flight and pace of the ball coming towards him and ended up paying the penalty.

Whatever the reason, he is trying desperately to redress the damage. He certainly could not get any lower and his racket has literally scooped under the ball to lift it steeply. If his opponent is at the net, this lobbed shot, instinctively invented, could just cause enough problems to effect a breathing space for recovery. It's a case of where there's life, there's hope!

COMMON FAULTS
1 Panicking completely and taking your eye off the ball.
2 Jerking upwards in a desperate attempt to push the ball over the net.

HOW TO PLAY
1 This is a 'You got yourself into this, now get yourself out' situation. You must rely and react on the ideas that immediately spring to mind.
2 Everything will happen so quickly that instinct will play the shot for you. Just make sure that you bring into play your emergency rules:
● no backswing
● firm grip on racket
● forward thrust with racket head
● stay calm.

Martina Navratilova and Pam Shriver
Doubles – supporting

The definition of the game of doubles is togetherness. Complete understanding between your partner and yourself is essential if you are going to master the art of doubles. For an art it is, and it does not follow that because you are a high-ranking singles player, you will automatically play top-class doubles.

However, there is no argument over the success of the Shriver/Navratilova partnership. Any team that can notch up over one hundred international doubles victories in succession must be worth analysis. Here Martina watches as Pam reaches for a high backhand volley. There has been no confusion over who should take this shot, even though Martina appears to be level with and quite close to her partner. She remains on her toes, aware that if Pam's shot is not a winner, she may well be able to step in and finish the point.

Note that Pam is right-handed and Martina left-handed. This is a good mixture if used correctly. Two forehands on the outside provide solidity but two backhands down the middle can cause confusion. But there need be no clashes if either partner calls her readiness to take a centrally placed ball.

COMMON FAULTS
1 Getting angry with yourself and shutting out your partner's help.
2 Getting anxious and failing to cover your half of the court, especially the down-the-middle ball.

SUPPORTING TACTICS
1 Stay keen and alert beside your partner, to create mutual confidence.
2 Talk between points. Offer a word of encouragement, suggestion or sympathy. Be understanding.
3 Cover your side of the court as completely as you should.
4 Do not be in too much of a rush to finish the rally yourself. Work with your partner to build up the understanding of your two games, so you can find ways of combining shots which will lead to an easy winner for *one* of you.
5 Each of you will have different strong points. Find ways of using them.
6 Never forget that you are only half of the partnership. You are obliged to give 100 per cent effort every time you go on court.
7 Never publicly blame your partner for a loss. You are a team and have to accept the rough with the smooth.

John McEnroe and Peter Fleming
Doubles – covering

Sometimes you are so eager to seek the volley at the net that when a lob goes up, you can be caught wrong-footed. That is when your partner can come to your rescue.

At other times a ball can be hit so high and deep that the best policy is to move back with it, let it drop and, depending on the height of its bounce off the ground, play either a groundstroke or a bouncing smash.

This is the situation here. Fleming has been lobbed down his line. The ball is very high and will bounce close to the sidelines, deep in the back court. McEnroe has moved back with him, ready to take the ball should his partner decide that he is not in a good position to attempt it.

It does look as if Fleming has this one under control and should be happy to hit the ball. He seems to be shaping up for a bouncing smash, to keep the ball low to the net and give a difficult volley to the opposing pair, who should have moved to the net. If McEnroe goes for this ball it means putting his own partnership on the defensive, as, being left-handed, his return would probably be a backhand lob. As it is he will see that Fleming is well-placed and will break away to assume a ready position towards the back of the court to await developments.

Neither partner will want to hang about at the back of the court however. All their instincts will be geared to moving back on the offensive as soon as possible. The knowledge of when to move up and down the court in unison comes with practice.

All in all the game of doubles is an enjoyable event for all standards. It is comforting to know that someone is helping on your side and covering half a court is far less enervating than playing the full singles area.

John Fitzgerald and Pat Cash
Doubles – net play

Here's a situation where togetherness is working beautifully. The middle of the court is always the danger area in doubles, with the question mark on who should take the ball. John Fitzgerald and Pat Cash are taking no chances and both have made ready for this shot. However, there is no problem as Cash is slightly behind his partner, able to see that Fitzgerald is in the better position and is going to get there first.

On the other hand, it could have happened that Fitzgerald did not reach the ball. Then Cash's back-up would have been indispensable.

You might think that Fitzgerald was close to 'poaching' the ball off Cash's racket. In fact, taking a ball which is not really yours (which is what 'poaching' means) is a rare occurrence in top-class tennis. It is more a dovetailing exercise based on the total understanding that each knows the other's capabilities exactly and is therefore quite happy with the partner's judgement.

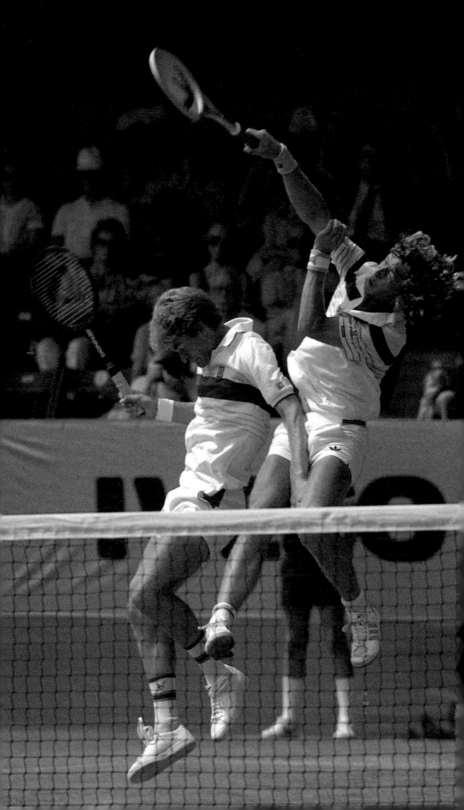

Anders Jarryd and Hans Simonsson
Doubles – sharing the court

This isn't quite the type of togetherness you need in doubles. What a horrible mess Anders Jarryd and Hans Simonsson have found themselves in, all because neither player called his intention.

The lob was obviously well-placed, high, down the middle of the court, tempting both men into going for it. By rights, a ball down the middle like this should be hit by the player in the left court (if he is right-handed) as that is his natural side for a smash.

To be aware of your partner's position on the court is essential. Complete understanding allows a partnership to move instinctively to cover the gaps. It is almost uncanny how some partners can read each other's intentions. This only comes with playing consistently together. Eventually you fit together like a jigsaw.

You may be unaware that you can call to your partner during a rally. Obviously there are times when an unexpected shout can be off-putting for the opposition and they may complain. Normally, however, a call of 'Yours', 'Mine', 'Out' or 'No' is acceptable. It is an integral part of doubles to warn or to instruct.

COURT STRATEGY

1 Do be aware of where your partner is on the court. Your back-up may be needed when there is trouble.
2 Do keep in contact all through a match. To be able to talk smooths difficult times and reinforces confidence.
3 Do call your intention to take a centrally placed ball. Otherwise injuries can result from a clash of bodies and rackets.
4 Do call your instruction. If you send up a short lob unintentionally call 'Back' to warn your partner of the need to defend against a probable heavy smash.
5 Do call if your partner is going back for a shot that is going out of court. When your partner runs backwards to smash a deep lob, for example, you may be better placed to see the exact position of a difficult ball.

John McEnroe and Peter Fleming

Doubles – intercepting

Probably the most exiciting match in tennis is a men's doubles with four expert players. The power, the touch, the speed; the close work between each pair trying to dominate the net position; the chance for the unexpected to happen; all combine to produce a mastery of tennis that is stimulating to watch. John McEnroe and Peter Fleming have a wonderful flair for doubles. Although McEnroe may be much higher in the world singles rankings than Fleming, on the doubles court they are equals and treat each other with respect.

With each man having confidence both in his own capabilities and his partner's, this pair produces the most spirited and courageous tennis. When everything is going well, picking off a winner seems ridiculously easy. It is in this situation that Fleming seizes the moment for a rapid and accurate interception at the net.

You must be wholly alert if you are going to intercept a volley at the net. Interceptions usually occur on the return of serve, when the receiver sends a ball cross-court. The move across the net must be made only at the last moment, though, otherwise you run the risk of the receiver noticing your intention and hitting the return down your outside line.

From this picture you can assume that McEnroe has served and has started his approach to the net. Then he has noticed Fleming moving across to intercept and has changed his direction to cross over behind his partner. When your partner goes for an interception, you must expect him to reach the ball and therefore your job is to cover the area he has left. Always try to anticipate where the ball might go and try never to be stranded in the same half of the court as your partner.

John Lloyd and Wendy Turnbull
Mixed doubles

The strategy for a mixed doubles partnership is essentially the same as that for men's or women's doubles, taking into account the relative imbalance in physical strength between the pair. Mutual confidence and communication are the keynote, as shown here in Wendy Turnbull's position at net while John Lloyd serves. She stands squarely midway between the centre line and the first sideline — not squeezed into the sidelines. She is not afraid that her partner will hit the back of her head with a fast first serve! This is a very rare occurrence in top-class tennis, but the wayward serve can be an unnerving hazard for club players.

Mixed doubles should not depend on the woman lobbing up balls from the baseline while her male partner throws himself around at the net. He may have the advantage of dominant strength, but the woman should be at the net whenever possible taking a part equal to her capabilities. Mixed doubles is a partnership where the power of the man's game is complemented by the guile of his partner.

The woman's game
- Do serve and volley and work close to the net. Staying back puts your partnership at a disadvantage.
- Do be bold enough to play your own game, but don't go for smashes when your partner's strength can do a better job.
- Pace your returns to make the most of your abilities. If your male opponent's serve comes down hard and fast, answer with a lob over the head of the female opponent.

The man's game
- Don't undermine your partner's confidence by showing impatience with any mistakes.
- Use your power to complement your partner's game, not to dominate it totally. Don't poach shots unnecessarily.
- Don't use brute force to intimidate your female opponent, such as slamming your service return at her body when she is standing at net. If you have no better strategy to win a point, your whole game needs improvement!

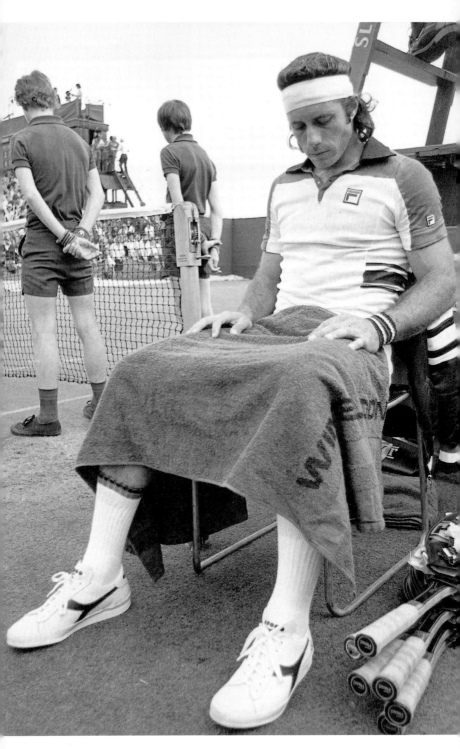

Guillermo Vilas

Mental and physical control

This is the calm before the storm of the next game. During this change over Court No.2 at Wimbledon is humming with the anticipation of the continuing match — but Guillermo Vilas is quite self-contained, directing his thoughts towards the working out of his tactics. He has one-and-a-half minutes to gather his thoughts and create a strategy to combat his opponent's strengths and exploit his weaknesses.

Even though it is summertime, he is taking no chances and has covered his legs with a towel to keep them relaxed. Warm legs will work harder and faster and will be less likely to cramp. This is a continuation of the physical preparation completed in the changing room before the match. He will have gone through a routine of stretching exercises to warm up his leg, arm and back muscles.

More and more often nowadays, tennis players find themselves a quiet corner where they can sit and relax to contemplate the coming match. To have a positive plan in mind before you go on court can only be better than giving way to pre-match nerves and rushing into the game unprepared. This is just as important to a club player as to a Wimbledon competitor. You want to be relaxed so you can play your best tennis. You want to think clearly. So give yourself a chance by putting everything else aside before you go on court.

Club courts may not run to the luxury of players' chairs by the side of the court, but that should not deter you from taking your time at the changeover. Towel down your legs and arms, change your sweatband, blow your nose or tie your shoe laces. All these things make you slow down and gather your wits. Aim at not being hustled, but do not break the rules by stalling for time.

John McEnroe v Chris Lewis
Wrong-footing your opponent

John McEnroe is a tactical genius. He has an
instinctive ability to work out the most
awkward place to put the ball. Here Chris Lewis
has decided that the ball is going down the line.
Wrong! John's intention is to send the ball

straight back to the position Chris has just left,
leaving him wrong-footed and floundering.
Watch out for an opportunity to make this play
when your opponent has started a little too
early in anticipation of your next shot.

Ken Rosewall
Playing on

Many players announce their retirement from tennis only to re-emerge a short time later muttering embarrassed explanations as to why they have decided to return to the fold. This doesn't only happen in world class circles, where cynics always assume the lure of the prize-money is the main reason for this revitalization.

There comes a time when the legs are not quite as youthful, the serve not quite as powerful, and recovery time from aching muscles is that much longer. That's the moment many players decide that enough is enough. But we may all be grateful that the current train of thought encourages tennis enthusiasts to play on indefinitely. There is absolutely no reason why age should be the criterion for giving up a game you love and from which you derive such pleasure. It is also a fact that playing sport keeps you youthful.

In recent years at club and national level, there has been a surge in the number of competitions for those in the higher age brackets — from 35 years and over up to the 65 and over veterans. An interesting phenomenon is the development of a monied circuit for former top players — such as Ken Rosewall, John Newcombe, Roger Taylor, Pancho Gonzales, to mention just a few who still play to a staggeringly high standard even though their first flush of youth is well behind them.

Maintaining your game
- Make sure your muscles are warm before you start playing.
- Play on just half the court. Plenty of exercise can still be gained.
- Always practise a few serves so that every muscle is used.
- Make sure your racket is the correct weight for you. A lighter one will probably be necessary, the older you get.
- Never play longer than you feel is right for you.

Bjorn Borg

Clay-court tennis

If a poll was taken among top players as to the
most demanding tennis surface, the consensus
would be clay, without any doubt. All players
dream of winning a title on the grass courts of
Wimbledon, but close on that, they would state
their desire to be victorious in the French Open
in Paris, on the continental clay courts of the
Stade Roland Garros. Why? Because clay
demands every facet of tennis skill:
● a calm temperament
● a clever head
● fleetness of foot
● total fitness
● talent and consistency.
Bjorn Borg was king in Paris as he combined all
these assets to wear down the resolve and
optimism of his opponents. He was prepared to
work all day on the slow surface even though it
meant covering a vast distance in court area.

Continental clay is a pleasant surface to play
on. As long as your shoes have sufficient grip,
the surface need not be intimidating. The knack
of clay-court playing is the ability to slide. Borg
was a master of the slide, the best way to take a
wide or short ball on a clay court.

Hints for clay-court play
1 Clay takes topspin and slice.
Topspin will bounce high; slice, low.
2 Long rallies from the baseline
should be expected.
3 To put the ball away for a winner on
clay demands patience to wait for the
correct ball and good tactics to work
your opponent out of position.
4 Clay negates power of shot, so use
angles, dropshots and loops instead.
5 Be prepared to work for each point.
Do not be in a hurry to approach the
net.
6 Stay calm and involved. Boredom
can creep in when rallies seem
interminable, so concentration on
tactics must remain solid.
7 Use the slide to reach wide or short
balls.
8 Learn to relax as you tumble, to
prevent injury.

Boris Becker
Playing on grass

On a grass court, Boris Becker will throw himself around as if he were made of rubber. He is not afraid of falling as he launches himself at an horizontal angle for a seemingly unreachable wide ball. This could be the impetuosity of youth, of course, but more likely it is confidence in his abilty to relax as he falls. This is a knack that not everyone achieves. Many are afraid of falling and instinctively tighten up as they feel their feet going from them. Ironically it is this rigidity that causes the injuries they fear.

If you must fall, a grass court is the best

Characteristics of grass-court play
1 It is a fast surface as the grass is cut very short and the surface is rolled to harden and compact it giving a reliable bounce.
2 Slice, topspin and flat shots are all effective in their own ways.

3 Grass is more suitable to an attacking player.
4 It is kind to the feet.
5 It demands speed, power, instinctiveness and touch.
6 The ball stays low as it speeds through.

surface. At least it is soft and yielding and injuries tend to be kept to a minimum. Grass courts are, unfortunately, dying out. The cost of upkeep is prohibitive and the vagaries of the weather can make the surface a lottery.

However, the Wimbledon lawns, coddled as they are from one Championship to the next, remain the mecca of tennis and rumours of their inevitable demise in favour of some synthetic surface are strenuously and vehemently rejected. Long may they be! For there is nothing better than playing tennis on a good grass court.

Hana Mandlikova

Synthetic outdoor courts

It used to be that three of the four Grand Slam Tournaments were played on grass — Wimbledon, the Australian Open and the US Open. The fourth, the French Open, has always been on continental clay.

Nowadays the US Open is played on a synthetic surface. It is like concrete, with cushioned layers below and painted layers on top. Depending on the number of layers, the pace of the courts can be altered. Most players would agree that the synthetic courts at Flushing Meadow are midway in pace between clay and grass and are fair to all types of player because of the regular bounce.

The Australian Open will now also change from grass to a synthetic surface at the new national complex where the tournament will be held.

Hana Mandlikova obviously approves of synthetic courts, having made a huge breakthrough in her own personal career by capturing the 1985 US Open singles title.

The advantages of synthetics
1 The upkeep is minimal.
2 The surface is acceptable to players of all standards.
3 Most synthetics drain and dry quickly after rain.
4 The surface gives a consistent bounce.
5 The surface tends to be cushioned so that legs are not jarred.

More and more tennis clubs are changing over to synthetic surfaces. Although they tend to be expensive to lay, they need very little maintenance and that is one of the requisites of the modern day tennis club. So many different synthetic surfaces are now on the market that the choice is quite overwhelming. It is an unenviable task to find the one that suits all particular needs and the decision must be carefully made. If your club is considering the changeover, seek advice, if possible, from your national tennis association.

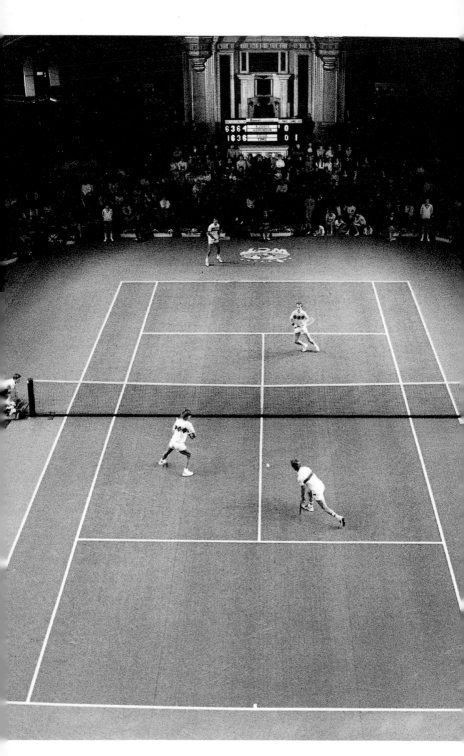

Anders Jarryd and Hans Simonsson
Tomas Smid and Pavel Slozil

Indoor surfaces

There must have been a few music composers turning in their graves when the Royal Albert Hall in London was first mooted as a venue for tennis. However this venerable old building has irrevocably become one of Britain's major indoor stadia.

It seems to bring out the theatrical in players. All seem to be more than ever imbued with the urge to perform well, as if to receive the applause of the very fabric of the building! They say the atmosphere is electric and certainly the closeness of the audience to the court gives a feeling on oneness, of all being involved in the struggle. But to watch tennis from a red velvet-covered Grand Loggia Box smacks of gracious living and that is borne out by the number of champagne corks that are popped during an evening session — much to the chagrin of the hard-working competitors!

To lay a tennis court at such a venue takes some organization. The sunken area in front of the stage has to be built up to a level with the first rows of the stalls to give sufficient length.

Synthetic surfaces laid indoors tend to be of a textile or carpet-type material and a shoe with too much grip can stick and cause an ankle to be turned. A shoe with a smoother sole is advocated for indoor play.

Hints for playing indoors

1 If the court is laid on a hollow frame, as in the Royal Albert Hall, the court will play faster than one laid on a solid base.

2 Strong lights are an unavoidable hazard. Make sure the toss of your serve is away from a direct beam.

3 Don't be lulled into hitting the ball too hard. Indoor tennis gives the impression of speed and power and can flatter you into thinking you are playing better than you actually are.

4 Do use attacking play on an indoor court.

Choosing Equipment

The choice of a tennis racket is a very personal thing. Rackets are available in every shape and size nowadays and really the only way to find one that suits you is by picking up various models and swinging them round. Older players tend toward the large head, lighter weight model, whereas the younger set favours the mid-head, composite racket that allows whip and spin. Rackets are available in different weights and various lengths, from cut-down, lightweight sizes for little ones starting out to the heavier types for adults, and there is a wide price range.

What to look for in a racket

● Make sure the racket is not too heavy for you. It should feel like a natural extension of your arm and should not tire your wrist.

● Ensure that the handle is not too large for your hand.

● The racket head should not feel heavy. If it does, it means that the balance of the racket itself is head-heavy.

● Swing the racket carefully to get the feel of it and only decide to buy when you are absolutely certain that it is the right one for you. The wrong choice can be expensive in more ways than one, causing injuries to wrist, elbow and shoulder.

● Short tennis sets are available and recommended for children from five years of age upwards. These comprise small, light rackets with a soft ball and give tinies the chance of learning the correct strokes of tennis at a very young age without fear of injury from heavy equipment. As they grow older and stronger, the children automatically move on to more regular equipment.

Shoes

The amount and variety of movement in tennis means that supportive, well fitting shoes are important. Keep in mind the following:

- The number one stipulation is that your shoes must be comfortable and must support the feet. Do take along a pair of your sport socks when you go to buy a pair of tennis shoes.
- For clay courts — a shoe with a good gripping sole is necessary.

- For grass courts — there is now a shoe with pimples on the sole for a better grip which does not tear up the court.
- For synthetic or indoor courts — you need a smoother sole so your foot has a certain amount of slide.
- Do not choose a shoe which has too thick a sole. This tends to raise you too high off the ground and leads to ricked ankles and pulled ligaments.

Preparation

Many tennis players keep their equipment in the back of the car and go straight from the office to the courts. The sedentary activities of desk work and driving make you a prime target for injury problems unless you loosen up before starting to play — and you may not realize this because stiffness and muscle strain will not manifest themselves until the next day.

All your muscles are interdependent, but tennis exercises some more than others. You must look after all the muscles to minimize the chances of common sporting injuries — especially in back and shoulders. If you are over 35 you may find that your muscles are gradually losing their tone. The triceps (at the back of the arm), for example, get flabby and it is a little more difficult to bend and stretch.

As well as following the all-round fitness plan described in the next few pages, do some limbering up before each practice session. Jog slowly around the court two or three times. Do some arm circling to get the important shoulder joints loosened up. Do a few stretching exercises (see page 115) and then jog another circuit of the court. After that, you will be tuned up and ready to play.

Preparation for a match should include not only a physical workout of this type, but also a period of mental preparation when you can clear your mind and think of your match strategy. Before you go to the court, find a quiet place where you can privately relax and concentrate. And don't forget the importance of staying cool on court, taking time between games, and even between points, to collect your thoughts and wind down when you are under pressure (see page 93). You are allowed 30 seconds between points and one-and-a-half minutes when changing ends.

Fitness Plan

The routine workout

There was a time when it was thought that the best way to get fit was to play a sport. However, for many sports you need first to be fit to play them satisfactorily, and tennis is a prime example. What's more, this is a 'one-sided' sport. Because the racket is always held in the same hand, one arm is consistently more heavily exercised than the other and this can lead to niggling pains and strains caused by imbalance in muscle use.

This fitness plan is designed to get you in trim, with a routine for all-round fitness and special exercises of particular benefit to tennis players. It is effective, but does not take up too much time, so it can put you in peak condition without diverting the energy you wish to put into playing your sport.

The basic 8-week plan

This consists of three types of activity: pattering and stretching, which occupy a few minutes daily, and additional aerobic exercise, to be fitted into your timetable six days a week.

Pattering is a simple but highly effective way of giving your heart and lungs a thorough workout without putting a strain on your knees and ankles. It also increases agility and speeds up reactions. It is similar to running on the spot but you *do not* lift your knees as if taking running steps. Your feet should barely leave the floor as you patter on the spot as fast as you can.

A fast patter means moving your feet at a rate of about 5 times a second. A few seconds of this pace and a further slower period and you've had enough after a mere minute or so. You'll feel a tightening of the calf muscle at the back of the lower leg at first. This will soon go away.

Stretching is slowly being recognized as one of the most vital ways of both avoiding injury and maintaining the natural spring of your muscles. A simple set of stretching exercises is included here that you can use daily to give your main muscle groups a good workout.

Ease into the stretch, going to the limit of discomfort, holding it a few seconds and then relaxing. Ignore those bouncy enthusiasts who exhort you to leap up and down like a Jack-in-the-Box. *Stretch gently,* like a cat waking up.

Aerobic exercise is slow but sure, the sort of exercise that takes a bit of time but doesn't leave you gasping for breath. It is sustained exercise which causes you to breath deeply and take in oxygen and does not necessarily imply the type of exhaustive routine followed in the modern trend of aerobics classes. The following activities are all aerobic exercise and you can choose one or a combination of any or all as part of your fitness routine.

Walking Set a target; the corner of the street, around the block, to the post office and back. Move briskly and with purpose. Don't combine this with carrying the shopping or stopping to look around.

Jogging/running As above, map out a route and follow it purposefully. Alter the route frequently if you are inclined to lose interest in running for its own sake.

Swimming Swim lengths or widths of a pool and combine this with static in-water exercises, such as holding the side rail and kicking your legs, or hooking feet to the side rail and moving your arms.

Cycling Build up pace and distance gradually as you get fitter.

Dancing Find a class with music you enjoy and people you like, that offers a comprehensive sequence of moves to work on the whole body.

Pace An important part of exercising is quality, not quantity, so the fitness plan suggests only a brief time for each form of exercise. To find out how fast you should go, use the 'talk test'. If you cannot chat to yourself as you work out, you are breathless from working too fast. As you get fitter, you will be able to accommodate a faster pace. This is just as useful as increasing the time you spend.

When to exercise

Use the chart to timetable the routine to your own lifestyle. Take the exercise when your body feels comfortable. Some of us are naturally morning people while others feel more lively in the evening. In fact, you could fit the whole routine into your lunch hour or carry out the pattering and stretching in the morning, the aerobic session at midday or after work.

How to exercise

Remember that exercise is meant to improve your condition, not become an additional strain. Use the following guidelines to make the best use of the fitness routine.

Check with your doctor before embarking on the fitness plan if
● you are over 40
● you have high blood pressure
● you have heart/bone/joint disease
● you suffer from chest pains

Once you start, don't train with friends and family. This tends to turn into competitive rather than shared activity, which puts you under unnecessary stress.

Warm up before doing an exercise routine (and before going out to play tennis). Your muscles need oxygen to function efficiently, whatever your degree of fitness, and you will exercise or play better if you're warmed up. What's more, you will lessen the chance of aches, pains and injuries.

After playing or exercising, wind down gently. Never stop suddenly. This also applies *during* exercise. If you feel dizzy, faint or suddenly fatigued, don't immediately flop to the floor or on to a chair — keep moving but slow down gradually to allow your body to change gear.

Maintaining fitness

When you are really pressed for time on your fitness routines, work on the principle 'anything is better than nothing'. Do keep up the daily pattering and stretching even if you cannot fit in aerobic exercise six days a week. Always patter first to ensure that oxygen-rich blood is pumping around your body before you stretch your muscles. Do the 5-minute workout whenever your body feels happiest — or better still, twice a day, once in the morning and once in the evening.

Pattering Follow the pace and timing shown on the chart for your age group (see over).

Stretching Hold each stretch for about 6 seconds. Do each stretch between 8 and 12 times, depending on how fit you feel.

Fitness Plan — 7-Day Routine

DAY	1	2	3	4	5	6	7
PATTERING	1-2 mins daily — increase pace weekly as below						
STRETCHING	Repeat the six exercises daily.						
AEROBIC	5 mins	8 mins	10 mins	15 mins	15 mins	REST	20 mins

Age 15-25 Repeat the 7-day routine over 8 weeks		**Age 26-35** Repeat the 7-day routine over 16 weeks		**Age 36-50** Repeat the 7-day routine over 24 weeks		**Age 50+** Repeat the 7-day routine over 32 weeks
WEEKS 1-2	I	WEEKS 1-4	I	WEEKS 1-3	I	WEEKS 1-4
30 secs slow		20 secs slow		15 secs slow		5 secs slow
15 secs fast	N	10 secs fast	N	10 secs fast	N	5 secs fast
30 secs slow	C	20 secs slow	C	15 secs slow	C	5 secs slow
WEEKS 3-4	R	WEEKS 5-8	R	WEEKS 4-6	R	WEEKS 5-8
30 secs slow		30 secs slow		20 secs slow		5 secs slow
30 secs fast	E	15 secs fast	E	10 secs fast	E	10 secs fast
30 secs slow	A	30 secs slow	A	20 secs slow	A	5 secs slow
WEEKS 5-6	S	WEEKS 9-12	S	WEEKS 7-12	S	WEEKS 9-12
30 secs slow		30 secs slow		30 secs slow		10 secs slow
45 secs fast	E	30 secs fast	E	15 secs fast	E	10 secs fast
30 secs slow		30 secs slow		30 secs slow		10 secs slow
WEEKS 7-8	P	WEEKS 13-14	P	WEEKS 13-18	P	WEEKS 13-16
30 secs slow		30 secs slow		30 secs slow		20 secs slow
60 secs fast	A	45 secs fast	A	30 secs fast	A	10 secs fast
30 secs slow	T	30 secs slow	T	30 secs slow	T	20 secs slow
	T	WEEKS 15-16	T	WEEKS 19-21	T	WEEKS 17-20
	E	30 secs slow	E	30 secs slow	E	30 secs slow
	R	60 secs fast	R	45 secs fast	R	15 secs fast
	I	30 secs slow	I	30 secs slow	I	30 secs slow
	N		N	WEEKS 22-24	N	WEEKS 21-24
	G		G	30 secs slow	G	30 secs slow
				60 secs fast		30 secs fast
				30 secs slow		30 secs slow
	P		P		P	WEEKS 25-28
	A		A		A	30 secs slow
	C		C		C	45 secs fast
	E		E		E	30 secs slow
						WEEKS 29-32
						30 secs slow
						60 secs fast
						30 secs slow

Calf muscle stretch

Stretch out your arms and lean forward with your hands flat against the wall. Keeping feet together and toes pointing forwards, press your hips forwards without bending your knees. Hold the stretch when you feel the pull on your calf muscles.

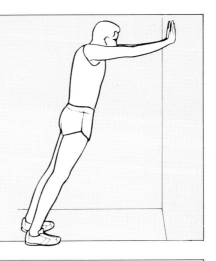

Hip rotation

Put your hands together and lean forward against a wall, with one leg in front of the other. Push out your hip on the side of the back leg and hold for 10 to 20 seconds. Reverse the position of the legs and repeat on the other side.

Trunk rotation

Stand with feet apart and planted in line with your shoulders. Clasp your fingers in front of you with elbows out to the sides. Turn from the hip, pushing back as far as possible to one side without moving your feet. Repeat to the other side.

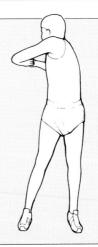

Adductor (inner thigh) stretch

Stand upright with feet apart. Keeping your upper body straight, bend one knee forward and hold the stretch when you feel a pull in the straightened leg. Repeat, bending the other leg forward.

Hamstring stretch

From a standing position bend right forward from the hips, letting your arms hang loosely. You will feel tension at the back of your thighs. Hold the position for 10 to 20 seconds, trying to relax through the tension.

Calf, quadriceps and hip stretch

Stand upright with hands on hips and lunge forward, behind your front leg and dropping your weight onto it. You should feel a 'pull' in the thigh of your rear leg. Hold the stretch for 10 seconds. Return to upright position and repeat with the other leg forward.

Tennis Fitness Exercises

Once you have raised your general level of fitness, you need to work on the specific areas of your body most exercised in tennis. But note that in serving, for example, you use virtually every muscle in your body from the arms, through the shoulders and back, right down to your feet. Therefore, *all* the muscles need to be exercised and strengthened and that is why it is important to maintain your overall tone and fitness, as well as exercising your racket hand and arm or your leg muscles.

The fitter you are the better chance you have of staving off the onset of fatigue. As you tire, so your muscles react more slowly, throwing out your timing. How often have you seen a deciding set won because one player had greater stamina?

You can use all of these exercises or work on the weaker areas of your body. No gymnasium is needed; do them at home, in the office or on the way to work.

GRIP EXERCISE
Strengthens wrist and forearm

Lessens/prevents occurrence of wrist and elbow problems

Use a ball, the size of a tennis ball but softer. Squeeze it 12 times in each hand. Hold each squeeze for 5 full seconds. Do not overdo this as you could then *cause* forearm problems. Build up to a maximum of 20 squeezes a day, over about four weeks.

PRESS UPS

Strengthen arms, shoulder and chest muscles

Lessen/prevent incidence of shoulders and high back pains

With all press ups, breathe out as you go down; breathe in as you come up again. Go up and down — *don't* hold the bent arm position.

Move from exercise 1 up to exercise 3 as you increase in strength and fitness. Start with the first exercise and do 8 each day. Work up to 20 a day after about four weeks. Then move up to the second exercise, then to the third. 20 a day is quite sufficient for exercise 3.

1 Kneel on all fours, arms shoulder-width apart, hands placed slightly in front of shoulders. At first, just touch forehead to floor. When stronger, move hands further forward and touch chest to floor. This is quite easy as your hands and knees take the weight when you push up.

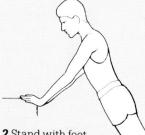

2 Stand with feet apart and lean against a solid table, gripping the edge with arms shoulder-width apart. Body and legs should be in a straight line. Do push ups so your chest touches table.

3 Do proper press ups, supported on your hands and toes with knees and torso leaving the floor. Keep your back straight and head in comfortable position, not thrust back awkwardly.

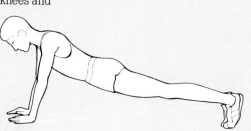

ABDOMINAL EXERCISE
Strengthens
abdominal muscles

Together with Neck
and Shoulder
exercises, prevents
back complaints,
particularly lower
back

Move from exercise 1 up to exercise 3
as you increase in strength and
fitness.

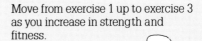

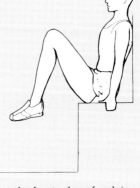

1 Lie flat on your back, arms by your side. Bring your knees up into a comfortable bend. Lift your head, shoulders and upper back slightly off the ground. Do 8 times a day. Build up to 20 times a day over about four weeks.

2 Sit on the front edge of a plain, kitchen-type chair. Grip the sides of the chair, just behind your body. Lean back so that your shoulders touch the back of the chair. Now try to touch your kneecaps to your forehead, bringing both your head forward and your legs up. Do 8 times a day. Build up to 20 times a day over about four weeks.

3 Lie on your back, arms by your sides and do the traditional 'sit up', trying to touch your toes. Do 5 times a day. Build up to 20 times a day over about four weeks.

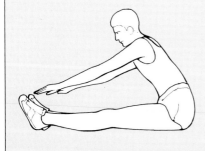

NECK AND SHOULDER EXERCISES

Strengthen neck, shoulders, upper back

Lessen/prevent aches and pains in neck, shoulders and triceps strain

Do each of these exercises 6 times, holding each push or pull for 5 seconds. Build up to a maximum of 20 a day, after about four weeks.

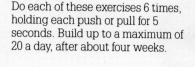

1 With elbows out horizontally, place hands on forehead. Try to push your head backwards with your hands, at the same time pushing forwards with your head.

3 With elbows out horizontally, grip hands together. Then try to pull them apart.

2 With elbows out horizontally, clasp hands behind head. Push forwards with hands, backwards with head.

4 With elbows out horizontally, put the palms of your hands together. Push them together hard.

LEG EXERCISES
Strengthen 'quads',
the big group of
muscles on front of
thigh
**Take stress off knee
joint, minimizing
injury**

All leg muscles except quadriceps
are well-catered for by pattering and
aerobic exercise of your choice
though cycling *does* workout this
important muscle group.

1 Standing up or lying in bed, try to
press knee 'backwards' with leg in
straight position. Hold press for
10 seconds. Build up to 50 a day.

2 Do short 'shuttle runs' over 5 yds
(5m) where you sprint, bend down
and pick up small bean bag, heavy
plastic bottle — any object that's
easy to pick up and weighs about
2 lbs (1 kg). Do 6 times. Build up to
20, even 30 over a month. This not
only lessens the occurrence of knee
injuries but is also good for the lower
back and for general agility.

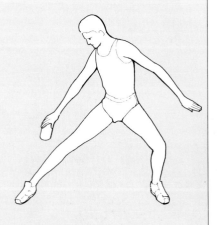